The following are just a few of the organizations Dr. Bart has helped:

Financial Services

- Bank of Montreal
- TD Canada Trust
- Deloitte & Touche
- CFO Financial Executives Forum
- Australian Society of Accountants
- State Farm Insurance

Health Care

- Ontario Hospital Association
- BC Health Leaders Forum
- Trillium Health Centre
- Credit Valley Hospital
- McMaster University Medical Centre
- The Griffin Centre

Government

- Treasury Board Secretariat
- Canadian Embassy, Washington, D.C.
- Nova Scotia Public Service Long Term Disability Plan
- Saskatchewan Research Council
- The Corporation of the Town of Oakville
- Office of the Superintendent of Financial Institutions

Services and Manufacturing

- ArcelorMittal Dofasco
- SAP
- Kraft Foods
- CBC Inc.
- CarSTAR Collision Service
- Apple Auto Glass

Human Resources

- Human Resources Professionals Association
- Canadian Human Resource Planners
- International Air Transport Association
- Conference Board of Canada
- Ontario Pharmacists' Association
- Association of Canadian Port Authorities

Education

- University of Western Ontario
- McMaster University
- University of Waterloo
- Mount Saint Vincent University
- Canadian Assoc. for Co-operative Ed.
- University of North Texas

20

ESSENTIAL QUESTIONS

CORPORATE DIRECTORS
SHOULD ASK ABOUT STRATEGY

and Workbook

Dr. Chris Bart, FCA

*The world's leading authority
on mission and vision statements
and their successful implementation*

Author of the highly acclaimed CICA publication,
20 Questions Directors Should Ask About Strategy, 2nd Edition

For Madeleine, Veronica, and Miriam
with love

Dr. Chris Bart, FCA
Corporate Missions Inc.
1063 King Street West, Suite 230
Hamilton, ON Canada L8S 4S3
905-308-8455
chrisbart@corporatemissionsinc.com
www.corporatemissionsinc.com

ISBN: 978-0-9732247-6-4

Design and composition by John Reinhardt Book Design

"Today's Boards are being held increasingly accountable and legally responsible for corporate action and inaction as a result of regulation and activist shareholder groups represented by concentrated ownership in the hands of hedge funds and private investors. Chris Bart's guide to Board processes for the 21st century, focussing on a Board's strategy execution, is the result of personal experience overlaid with academic insight into these formidable challenges. A invaluable tool for incumbents and aspiring candidates for for-profit and not-for-profit Board service."

AUSTIN BEUTEL
Chairman, Oakwest Corporation Ltd., and the Equitable Group/Equitable Trust Company,
Director, Aecon Group, Astral Media and Opta Minerals,
Co-founder & Past Chairman, Beutel Goodman & Company
Co-founder, Dynamic Mutual Funds Group
Past Chairman, Sunnybrook Health Sciences Centre

• • •

"Most directors struggle with the approach they should take to their corporation's important task of strategic planning. This work gives directors a succinct and useable toolkit to help in that task."

NANCY E. HOPKINS, Q.C., (HON) C.A.
Partner, McDougall Gauley LLP
Director & Chair, Nominating, Governance & Risk Committee, Cameco Corporation
Chair, University of Saskatchewan
Director & Chair, Audit Committee, Growthworks Canadian Fund Inc.
Director & Chair, Governance Committee, Canada Pension Plan Investment Board

• • •

"The importance of corporate governance today simply cannot be overstated and *The 20 Essential Questions Directors Should Ask About Strategy* is a great way to help frame the role of the Director in today's business environment. Like any framework it cannot be completely definitive, however, developing answers to these questions, and the additional clarifying questions they are likely to solicit, should provide any Director with a basis for addressing his/her role in the corporate governance structure of the organization as it relates to the crucial area of Strategy for any enterprise."

BRUCE REID
Director, The Faithshire Financial Corp., Lynx Equity Ltd., Direct Access Marketing Inc.,
ThoughtSpeed Inc., Cornerstone Equestrian Center Ltd., and The Richard Ivey School of Business
Past Chairman, Sybase Canada Inc, W.H. Smith Canada Ltd. and Midnorthern Group Inc.,
The Retail Council of Canada, and The Credit Valley Hospital Foundation

• • •

"*20 Essential Questions Corporate Directors Should Ask About Strategy* should be mandatory for all Board members. It is a very practical guide for becoming an effective and productive Board member."

DON ZIRALDO, CM, LLD
Founder, Inniskillin Wines, Chairman, Ziraldo Icewines,
Director, Mobilotto Inc, Shaftesbury Films inc.,
Vineland Innovation and Research Centre

"*20 Essential Questions* should be compulsory reading for all board directors. Bart deals with the critical subject of strategy in a concise, focused, and comprehensive manner. It's everything that needs to be asked about strategy, made simple."

• • •

"Succinctly identifying the needs of corporate board, this publication of 'strategic questions' is an important, relevant and timely reminder to all Directors and Senior Management of the explicit responsibilities and accountabilities for organizational strategy."

• • •

"*20 Essential Questions Directors Should Ask About Strategy* is a practical, plain language tool to help directors of both large and small organizations to understand, assess and monitor strategy."

• • •

"A prominent paradox in contemporary corporate governance is the wide awareness among directors of their duty, under legislation and suggested best practices, with respect to active oversight of the strategic planning process in their organizations, while at the same time rating themselves less than effective in actually meeting this responsibility. One reason behind this paradox is uncertainty about how to practically engage the discussion with management and how to determine who should bear which responsibilities as the planning process develops and unfolds. This 3rd edition, like its predecessors, gives directors an appropriate point of departure and a sure course to steer in navigating this most important subject. To the extent that the principal duty of every director is to ask informed and relevant questions, these questions assist all of us in meeting our fiduciary obligations."

• • •

"Chris has managed in this focused 20 questions monograph and workbook, to capture the essence of the link between strategy and governance. In a practical and thought provoking way, he challenges us to think and ask questions about where we have been, where we are going and why we think going there is the right thing to do"

ANTHONY GIOVINAZZO, C.DIR.
President & CEO, Cynapsus Therapeutics Inc.

• • •

"As a serious long serving Director of several successful large private and public companies, I congratulate Chris Bart on providing a succinct road map for directors to monitor one of the most important elements of their job as a responsible Director. Canada is a world leader in good corporate governance and Bart's *20 Essential Questions* add immensely to this body of work."

J. LORNE BRAITHWAITE
President & Chief Executive Officer, BUILD TORONTO INC
Founder, Chairman, President & CEO, Cambridge Shopping Centres
Past Worldwide Chairman, International Council of Shopping Centres
Chair, Investment Advisory Committee, Canada Post Pension Plan
Director, Enbridge Inc. and Bata Shoe Corporation Worldwide

• • •

"Ensuring an organization has an optimal strategy is a key board responsibility. Following the line of critical questioning and critical thinking outlined in *20 Questions Directors Should Ask About Strategy* will go a long way to satisfying the board's role in establishing an appropriate strategic direction."

DON MCCREESH
President, The Garnet Group
Chair, Educators Financial Group
Past Board Chair and Chair of the HR Committee, Brainhunter Inc.
Former Lead Director and Past Chair of the Corporate Governance and HR/Compensation Committees, RAND A
Technology Corporation
Past Chair, Imagine Canada and YMCA Canada

• • •

"A Must Read! — a concise and relevant reminder of the content to keep in mind when planning any corporation's strategy."

LESLIE MARKOW, CA, CPA
Director and Audit Committee Chair, Jemtec Inc.

• • •

Contents

Preface

HOW DO CORPORATE DIRECTORS fulfill their governance responsibilities in a complex and evolving regulatory environment? How do they contribute to the development and sustainability of successful organizations? Answer: *they must ask intelligent, informed questions of management and of themselves.*

This monograph is designed to help members of corporate boards (both publicly listed and privately owned) fulfill their responsibility for contributing to the development of their organization's strategic direction and for approving and monitoring the strategic plan. It is intended primarily to help individual directors, but boards may also wish to use it for orientation and discussion.

The role of corporate directors sometimes includes actually formulating the company's strategic plan—especially where smaller scale organizations are concerned. More often though, when sufficient management resources are available, it involves participating with management to help set the mission, vision and values and then constructively engaging with them to gain reasonable assurance (by asking enough of the right kinds of questions) that the rest of the plan has been properly developed and is, in fact, plausible. This monograph provides suggested questions for a board to ask the CEO, senior management, professional advisors—and even itself. For each question there is a brief explanatory background.

Interestingly, the concepts, processes and principles first espoused in this publication in 2003 still appear to be applicable. More importantly, the questions are now "time tested" and, as such, have proven their ability to be helpful to readers not just in the past, but perhaps well into the future.

Chris Bart

How to Use this Publication

THIS PUBLICATION is designed to be a concise, easy-to-read introduction to the role that directors play in performing one of their most important functions—**helping to set the strategic direction of the organization.** The question format reflects the oversight role of directors, which includes asking management—and themselves—questions to fulfill their primary fiduciary responsibility i.e. **to act in the best interests of the organization and *all* of its stakeholders, not just one or more selected stakeholder groups.** Unfortunately, in the past, not all directors felt comfortable in asking questions in the boardroom, often because they didn't know what types of questions to ask—and which ones were even permissible.

Accordingly, the questions presented here offer guidance to corporate directors on frameworks, processes and outcomes in order both to provide them with insight and to stimulate discussion on the important topics related to strategy. These questions, however, are not intended to be a comprehensive checklist—they are merely a starting point. *But, they are also questions for which the answers should be known by every corporate director.*

It should be pointed out that asking these questions directly of management may not always be the preferred course of action. In such circumstances, then, the board should ask management to prepare briefings that address the salient points raised by the questions.

Finally, the comments that accompany the questions in this monograph are intended to provide directors with a basis for critically assessing the answers they are given and for digging deeper if necessary. The comments summarize current thinking on the issues and the practices of leading corporations. And while the questions can—and should—apply to any corporation, the answers will naturally vary according to the size, complexity and sophistication of each individual organization.

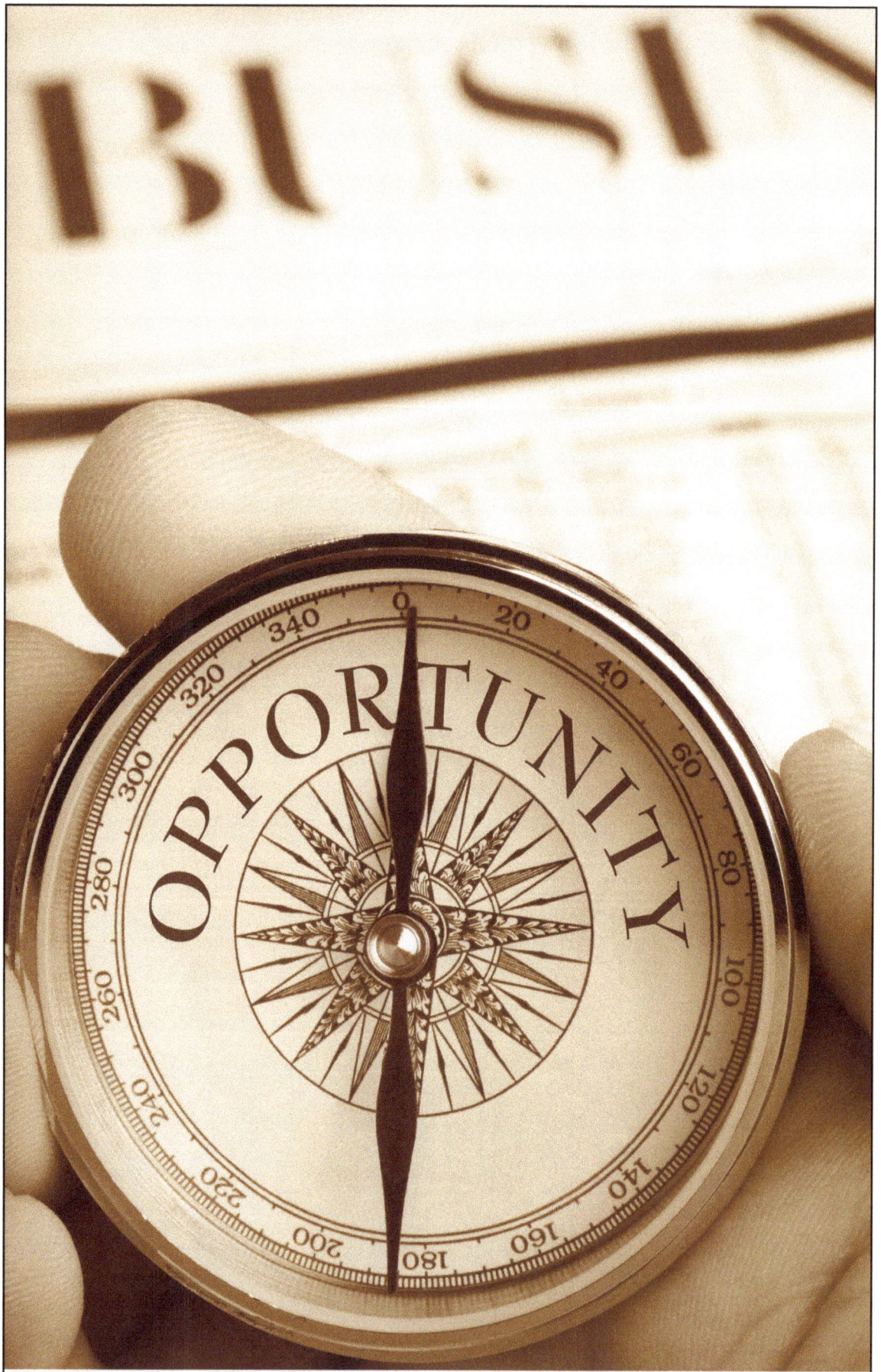

Corporate Directors and Strategy

THE NOTION of the board's responsibilities with respect to a corporation's strategic plan has, today, become no longer debatable. But what do these new responsibilities entail? And how should corporate directors exercise them?

At its most general level, a board's responsibility for strategy stems from the simple fact that *all* corporations are created to fulfill some purpose and that the people who contribute financially to the organization—the shareholders especially—want to feel confident that their financial support is not going to be squandered or misused.

Boards of directors, therefore, have been created to be the legal "stewards" of an organization and its property.

What this means in practical terms is that directors have been entrusted with the assets of the organization and, therefore, are responsible for their *safeguarding, enhancing their value and/or appropriately distributing them.* Stewardship also means, though, that boards are responsible for ensuring that the affairs of the organization are managed in accordance with its stated purpose either directly or by delegating this responsibility to one or more managers and then 'supervising' them.

Accordingly, directors need to be selected with care and their responsibilities need to be taken seriously. In particular, they should be selected on the basis of their ability to provide the organization with **oversight, insight and foresight.**

In terms of their 'oversight' function, directors must ensure that appropriate attention is given to the organization's strategy as well as identifying, managing and monitoring risks. The oversight role also involves providing for the smooth, effective and efficient functioning of the corporation.

With respect to their 'insight' role, corporate boards are expected to add their experience and wisdom to improve the organization's performance. Directors of smaller companies, for example, are sometimes required by necessity to take a more hands-on role such as when a director with financial expertise is also asked to serve as the organization's treasurer. On the other hand, when professional managers are in place, directors use their insight capabilities to supplement and enhance (but *not* second guess) executive decision-making.

As for 'foresight', corporations want their directors to provide a perspective on the future that helps the organization identify those opportunities that are most worth pursuing.

But, whether or not they delegate responsibility for managing the organization to others, the ultimate goal for corporate directors to seek in their pursuit of good governance is *the promotion of effective decision making.* Directors are there to make sure that the right decisions are made on a timely basis. And of all the decisions that a board might be called upon to make or approve, one of the most important concerns the selection of the organization's strategy.

Interestingly, the nature and degree of a board's actual participation in **creating, reviewing and approving** their organization's strategy will vary with the circumstances in which the directors find themselves.

For example, all privately owned corporations start out small in size and operate with an extremely focused mandate. In such circumstances the board and management are one and the same with the board performing many, if not all, of the organization's managerial functions. In these organizations, the board's responsibility for strategy involves both formulating the strategy and creating the written document that describes it—i.e., the strategic plan. And then there is the additional burden of developing a detailed operating plan and budget to bring the strategy to life.

On the other hand, boards of publicly listed corporations generally share their involvement in strategy with the professional managers who perform the day-to-day work of the corporation (and who also have the job of turning the strategy into an operating plan and then executing it). In these circumstances, the board's job is to lay down a structure and process that allows it to be *constructively involved* with management in both developing and approving the corporation's strategy.

Constructive involvement

A major consideration in becoming constructively involved concerns the specification of the division of responsibilities between the board and management for the various tasks undertaken to lead the organization. One recommended way of organizing a board's constructive involvement in relation to developing strategy is provided in Figure 1. This template, however, anticipates a corporation in which the board stays focused exclusively on strategic issues and leaves responsibility for operations exclusively in the hands of management.

In those corporations, where the directors have a more hands-on role in the day-to-day management of the organization, the board's operational responsibilities will increase and also trigger the need for the board to divide its operational and oversight responsibilities among its members.

For constructive involvement to be truly effective, however, a culture and climate of mutual respect and trust must exist between the board and senior management. This is something the board and management are both responsible for creating. For its part, the board contributes to building this culture by making sure that it participates in setting strategy in a cooperative rather than confrontational manner.

At the core of constructive involvement, however, is the role that directors perform through *the questions they ask either of management or of themselves*. By asking questions, ideally with fresh and unbiased eyes, directors aim to determine whether the organization:

- ✓ is on a proper course
- ✓ is conducting optimal decision making (as opposed to "satisficing" i.e., accepting decisions that are just "good enough")
- ✓ exercises sufficient creativity in its problem solving, and
- ✓ is appropriately administered and controlled.

But not just any questions will do. When it comes to strategy, directors must ask the *right* questions if they are to be effective in helping the organization set a future direction that will ensure its long-term survival. Indeed, doing so is the essence of all strategic planning efforts and the winning strategies that such planning efforts aspire to produce!

When developing a corporation's strategy, it is especially important that the board and management consider the specific needs of a wide range of **stakeholders**, including employees, customers, suppliers, and communities with particular attention to the owners (i.e. shareholders) of the organization. After all, it is those stakeholders' positive response to the strategy that is often critical to the corporation's success.

Figure 1 provides a framework for dividing the responsibilities for the corporation's strategy and strategic planning between the board and management. The precise division of responsibilities will depend on the corporation's size, complexity and resources, so each corporation should determine the allocation of planning responsibilities based on the nature of the organization, the composition of the board and any specific regulatory requirements.

FIGURE 1

Constructive Involvement: Roles and responsibilities of boards and management for strategic plans and planning

TASK	RESPONSIBILITY	
	Mgt.	Board
Developing a strategic planning process	X	
Assessing and approving the strategic planning process		X
Developing the mission, vision, and values (*)	X	X
Developing the objectives	X	
Assessing and approving the objectives		X
Identifying business arenas within which to achieve the objectives	X	
Assessing and approving the business arena selections		X
Data collection and analysis with respect to the strategic plan (See the Appendix)	X	
Preparing the written strategic plan	X	
Assessing and approving the strategic plan and management's ability to execute it		X
Scheduling strategic planning and strategy execution review meetings	X	
Preparing operating plans	X	
Preparing budgets	X	
Approving budgets		X
Preparing reports on the organization's strategy execution and accomplishment of strategic objectives	X	
Monitoring the execution of the strategy and its achievement		X
Approving changes to the strategy as warranted		X

* Traditional governance models restrict the board's involvement to reviewing and approving the mission, vision and values. However, recent research by the author suggests that superior organizational performance and innovativeness occurs when boards participate more actively in developing these strategic documents.

Questions Corporate Directors Should Ask About Strategy

THE FOLLOWING SET of **20 Essential Questions** represents a structured framework to help corporate directors fulfill their responsibilities for developing, assessing, approving, monitoring and changing their organization's strategy.

The nine questions in the first section, "In the Beginning...Understanding Strategy," will help directors develop a common understanding of strategy in the context of their own organization—**a strategic framework.** This provides the foundation needed for a more detailed discussion and assessment of their organization's strategy, using questions 10 through 20.

While the questions are presented in a particular order, individual directors may prefer to begin at different points within the framework.

It is strongly recommended, though, that directors consider all of the questions.

Finally, as with any major organizational undertaking such as determining the board's role in strategy, it is usually best to go slowly and to keep things simple. After all, most boards are usually currently involved with their organization's strategy in some fashion. Adjusting to the approach recommended here, though, may involve some major changes in the way that the board and individual directors conduct themselves. And that, in turn, may take some time to get right.

It is better to know some of the questions than all of the answers.

—James Thurber

In the Beginning...Understanding Strategy

The first question that every corporate director must ask in order to grasp their organization's strategy is:

1. How is strategy defined at this corporation?

While this question is easy to ask, agreeing on the answer is often difficult. Many different definitions of strategy exist and, as a result, directors often come to their organizations with different and competing versions of the term. When combined with management's own definitions, there is often much confusion and conflict as to what constitutes the proper description of an organization's strategy.

Rather than present and debate alternative definitions, this document has adapted one recent and contemporary description of strategy, which appears to strike the balance that many directors seem to be looking for. This definition contends that a corporation's strategy involves:

1. the articulation of those long term **goals** (i.e., mission, vision and values) and **objectives** which reflect:
   a. the relationship that the organization wishes to have with its different stakeholder groups and,
   b. in particular, how the organization intends to address important stakeholder needs to gain a competitive advantage; and
2. the specification of the **business activities** within which those goals and objectives are to be achieved.

While other definitions exist, this approach to strategy is easily understood by any director or senior officer. It answers the **essential questions** of strategy that should be of concern to every director, which are:

2. **What are we ultimately trying to accomplish (currently)— or where do we eventually want to get to? (The Vision Goal)**

3. **What is our current purpose—or, why do we exist? (The Mission Goals)**
   a. Who are the key stakeholders that have a significant impact on our business(es) and its sustainability (i.e. customers, employees, shareholders, suppliers, regulators, society-at-large, etc.)?
   b. What specific needs are we trying to satisfy better than our competitors for each of our key stakeholders in order to secure their long-term loyalty, commitment and support?

4. **What are the current internal ethical and cultural ("how we do things around here") priorities that attract stakeholders to us? (The Values Goals)**

5. **What are the specific measures and targets that we use to judge our progress in achieving our vision, mission and values goals? (The Objectives)**

6. **What specific products and/or services have we currently chosen to focus on and, to which specific customers (or markets) have we chosen to offer them for the purposes of achieving our objectives? (The Business Arenas)**

These detailed questions specify the *salient* components—vision, mission, values, objectives and scope of activities—that define and describe any organization's strategy in a **complete and comprehensive fashion**. Therefore, directors need to consider them both individually and as a group whenever they seek to describe the strategy for their particular corporation.

Interestingly, questions 2–6 are sometimes summarized through the more general query of "what business(es) are we in?" Recent experience suggests, however, that using such an approach may now be too vague to gain the sort of insights that directors are looking for.

Whatever approach is taken, though, *directors must agree among themselves and with management on how they will define and articulate their organization's strategy.*

This common understanding is necessary if everyone is to know clearly **which decisions are strategic, and which ones are not**. Failing to agree on the way strategy is defined and articulated usually results in poor communication, confusion and even conflict whenever the topic of the organization's strategy is raised. Therefore, one important contextual question that every director must ask early on with respect to assessing and approving the organization's strategy is:

If you don't know where you are going, you'll probably wind up someplace else.

—Anon.

7. **Is the definition and interpretation of the word "strategy", as described above in Questions 1 to 6, shared by all directors and management?**

With so many different definitions of the word "strategy" around, it is important for all of the directors and management in any company to share a common understanding of the term. Otherwise, they will have serious disagreements and misunderstandings as to what decisions are strategic (i.e. the ones that fall properly within the board's purview) versus which decisions are not (i.e. the operational ones belonging to management's discretion and decision making autonomy). Boards and their managements should therefore confirm that they have a common and precise definition of the term.

It is strongly recommended, however, that company directors adopt the definition of strategy provided above because experience has shown it to be very robust and capable of covering a variety of circumstances.[1] It can be used to describe any organization's strategy, whether it is one currently in place—or one being proposed for the future.

The definition of strategy prescribed in this document may also be used to describe two terms that are often used interchangeably, but which sometimes have quite different meanings in corporations: **the business strategy and the organizational (or overall) strategy.** Generally speaking, the distinction between these two concepts turns largely on the breadth and scale of a corporation's scope or domain of activities and operations.

More specifically, *a business strategy usually concerns a specific product or service that the organization offers to a specific type of customer in a defined location.* For most small companies, the scope or domain of operations is relatively narrow. Consequently, their 'business strategy' would be virtually the same as their 'corporate strategy'.

Larger organizations, on the other hand, may have a variety of different activities, with a distinct business strategy for each. Directors of large corporations with substantive, diversified activities, therefore, need to ask:

8. What are the major business strategies that make up the overall corporate strategy?

Over time, a corporation may provide new products or services or serve a different range of customers or markets. As a corporation expands its activities, multiple business strategies may come into play (each defined using the strategic components provided in questions 2 though 6). Taken together, these business strategies represent the *overall* organizational strategy. The organizational strategy, therefore, becomes something separate and distinct from the individual business strategies.

In organizations with multiple business strategies, the board should focus primarily on the corporate—or "overall"—strategy. It should only become involved with assessing and approving individual business strategies when they represent major changes to the organization's overall direction—such as, when a new major business activity is added/acquired or an existing one closed/sold. It is still advisable, though, that directors be periodically informed of and review the major business strategies of the corporation so they better understand the impact these have on the whole organization.

---

[1] The definition of strategy used in this monograph has been actively embraced by thousands of company directors attending the Chartered Director Program of the Directors College since 2003. It has also been successfully used by the author when advising boards and managements during consulting engagements or when facilitating a company's strategic retreat.

9. Do circumstances warrant the board's involvement in (i.e. reviewing, assessing and approving) the corporation's detailed operating plan?

The **operating plan** puts "flesh and bones" on a corporation's strategy. Typically, it addresses all of the major functional areas, such as marketing, sales, production services, finance and human resources. Therefore, developing such a plan involves considering a multitude of specific details and **action plans** (typically referred to as **tactics**) concerning the way the organization intends to achieve its mission, vision, values and objectives (given its choice of business arenas).

In large corporations, many staff members and individual departments normally contribute to developing the operating plan. It is a process that usually involves several functional experts and requires making innumerable decisions that typically go well beyond the knowledge, competence and time availability of most directors.

Consequently, the reason why boards of larger organizations should not get involved in the details of the operating plans is fairly straightforward: *this is what management is hired and paid to do.* The board should, therefore, diligently avoid reviewing, assessing and approving the details of the organization's operating plan.

Instead, directors should focus on specifying the guidelines (such as hurdle rates, threshold levels, and spending or policy limits) that will shape and affect the development of the operating plan. They should also ensure that operating plans are being carried out in a fiscally prudent manner as part of their normal oversight responsibilities. (For example, the board may do this through its review and approval of high-level strategic initiatives, the organization's budget and subsequent variance reviews.)

Except for these high level reviews and summary budget approvals, the responsibility for a large corporation's operating plan usually falls outside the board's normal governance responsibilities. However, there are still certain occasions when boards of large corporations may become actively involved in the organization's operating plan. One occurs when the organization faces a crisis and requires whatever benefit the board's collective wisdom has to offer. The other is when there is agreement *from* senior management concerning the board's involvement in this area.

Boards of smaller companies, on the other hand, face different circumstances. Their organizations may lack the necessary managerial strength or depth, so board members may be required to take a more a hands-on role in managing the organization, including the review of every aspect of operations. In some circumstances, these boards may assign certain directors the responsibility for actually working with management on the operating plan. However, it is imperative that these boards determine how they will also carry out their governance oversight roles. One way of doing this is by dividing various responsibilities among the directors with some having the job of providing oversight to those (other directors) who have been given the task of helping to create various aspects of the operating plan.

Assessing and Evaluating Strategy

The first step in assessing a corporation's strategy is to have it formally written down and communicated explicitly to all board members (ideally by answering Questions 2–6). This allows directors the opportunity to adequately reflect upon and ponder the *choices of goals, objectives and scope of business activities (i.e. products/services/customers/markets) imbedded within that strategy.*

Once the hurdle of describing and understanding a corporation's strategy has been navigated, the board and its directors are faced with their most important question:

10. Does this corporation have the right strategy and, if not, what should it be?

Every organization has a strategy, which may be either explicit or implicit. However, not every organization necessarily has a good one.

Given the board's responsibility for reviewing, assessing and approving the corporation's strategy, it is incumbent upon directors to do their utmost to ensure that their organization's strategy is the right one for it.

Usually, poor financial results are the first indicator that a corporation's strategy is not working. However, the major issue is whether the failure is due to bad formulation (the wrong strategy was chosen) or bad implementation (a good strategy is being poorly executed).

To determine whether the organization has the "right strategy", the board and its management need to ask and answer the following two seminal questions:

1. Does the marketplace potential (market size, growth, number of competitors, barriers to entry etc.) currently exist for us to achieve our financial and market share objectives given how we have chosen to attract and retain customers in our chosen business arenas? and
2. Does the company have the right resources in sufficient quantity to capture that potential and keep the competition at bay?

If the answer to both questions is "yes", then any performance problems are most likely related more to matters of strategy execution than strategy formulation. However, if the answer to either one or both questions is "no", there is most definitely a problem with the organization's choice of strategy and it needs to be reconsidered to take into account the realities of the current situation.

11. What process was used to formulate the strategy contained in the corporation's strategic plan and does the plan's document contain all of the proper information?

One of the first things to consider when attempting to determine the quality and appropriateness of a corporation's strategy is the way it was developed. Was the strategy developed through an orderly and thoughtful process? Or was it put together through "gut feel" and an "on-the-back-of-an-envelope" approach? Research has confirmed that organizations that follow an organized, structured planning process develop better strategies and achieve higher performance results, on average, than those that do not.

So what is *strategic planning*?

Simply put, **strategic planning is the process that helps establish the organization's strategy**. It results in a formal, written document, referred to **as the strategic plan**.

A good strategic plan sets forth:

✓ The reasons why the corporation's mission, vision, values and objectives were chosen

✓ The reasons why the organization's scope of business activities—and the markets it chooses to serve—are perceived to be the optimal choices for it to achieve its goals and objectives

✓ The major strategic alternatives that were considered and rejected by management in favor of the proposed strategy

✓ Assumptions made about the external environment that may affect the organization's ability to achieve its goals and objectives

✓ Assumptions made about the organization's own resources that may affect its ability to serve its external markets

✓ Assessments of the risks facing the organization and its strategic choices, and the way those risks are to be managed, and

✓ The rationale for all major organizational arrangements, such as structure, staffing and controls, which are necessary for the organization to execute its strategy.

The Appendix provides a more detailed list of the information that should typically be produced by a good strategic planning process.

The following nine questions are provided to help directors assess the quality of the strategy presented to them and the planning process used to develop it. Directors should be satisfied that each of these questions is sufficiently answered in the plan documentation.

It's not the plan that is important, it's the planning.

—Dr. Graeme Edwards

12. Does the strategy have the right vision?

Visions help provide a long-term direction to an organization and enhance its stakeholders' understanding of what the organization is ultimately trying to accomplish. Generally, visions are concerned with achieving greatness on one or more dimensions—be it market share, quality, revenues, profits, social outcomes, or admiration, to name just a few.

One of the most famous vision statements ever created was that of General Electric under the former leadership of CEO Jack Welch. The company's vision was: To become the most competitive enterprise in the world by being number one or number two in every business in which we compete.

A great vision is also often a short aspirational statement in which the ability—or way—to achieve it is neither readily apparent nor available. This is because the essential purpose of a vision is to describe a future state that is so desirable that it harnesses both the intellectual and emotional commitment of major stakeholders and makes them want to work passionately towards achieving it.

A notable example of an aspirational vision comes from the early 1960s, when US President John Kennedy challenged NASA to: "land a man on the surface of the moon and return him safely back to earth before the end of the decade." At the time, few people in NASA actually believed that was possible because it would require so many new technologies that had yet to be invented at that time. Nevertheless, Kennedy's vision so exited the scientists at the space agency about the prospects of actually making it happen 'during their watch' that they eventually fulfilled it.

By their nature as aspirational statements, great visions generally take a long time to realize. Like Kennedy's challenge to NASA in the 1960s, however, it is not unusual for a vision to take from 5 to 10 years to realize. Directors should, therefore, ensure that their organization's vision involves a suitable time frame for its achievement.

Finally, visions that are explicit, clear and widely shared have a powerful and positive impact on internal stakeholders (i.e. employees) and their behaviors. The more committed these individuals are to seeing their organization's vision achieved, the more their collective spirit will serve to reinforce desired behaviours and focus both individual and group efforts on achieving desired outcomes. Consequently, directors should assure themselves that their organization's vision is widely known, understood—and accepted—throughout the enterprise.

13. Does the strategy have the right mission?

A mission statement is a formal written document that describes an organization's unique and enduring purpose. In particular, it should answer the most fundamental question of organizational purpose: Why do we exist?

Generally speaking, organizations exist when they are able to continuously meet and satisfy the needs of those important *stakeholders* who have a significant influence on the organization and its sustainability. A corporation's stakeholders can include shareholders, customers, employees, suppliers, or even society-at-large. The more the organization identifies, meets and satisfies its stakeholders' needs *better than its competitors*, the more likely it will be able to attract and retain the long-term loyalty and support of each stakeholder and the greater the probability of the organization's ongoing success and prosperity.

Therefore, a corporation's mission is the essential platform that helps transport the organization towards its vision!

On the other hand, to the extent that a corporation fails to satisfy a particular stakeholder group in a significant way, it risks alienating the commitment of that group to the organization and, even worse, goading them into an attack. This will most likely result in the failure of one or more goals and objectives and, under extreme conditions, can even lead to problems in organizational survival.

Directors must, therefore, ensure that the mission statement **acknowledges the importance of multiple stakeholder groups** to the organization's long-term survival and that it **balances their often competing interests**. However, it is especially important that the stakeholder needs specified in the mission be grounded in *reality*. The strategic plan should indicate the basis upon which the needs of each stakeholder group were identified and selected (such as through surveys or informal focus groups).

Although various methods may be used to identify stakeholders and their needs, this does not need to be a long, complicated or expensive exercise. Instead, it should be designed to quickly confirm, or deny, the instincts or perceptions of the board and management with respect to stakeholder needs.

Finally, as is the case with an organization's vision, mission statements should be explicit, clear and widely shared if they are to have a powerful and positive impact on internal stakeholders' behaviours. Accordingly, directors need to assure themselves that people throughout the corporation are aware of, understand and accept the organization's mission.

14. Does the strategy have a proper statement of values?

Every organization needs to be sure that the actions and behaviours of its employees—in striving to maximize shareholder value and achieve performance targets—can withstand the test of public scrutiny.

Values constitute the internal ethical and cultural priorities that shape the way people behave and make decisions. When values, such as honesty, mutual respect, transparency, innovation, teamwork, commitment, sustainability, etc., are widely shared, they enhance the organization's ability to focus the behaviour of its employees. Corporations can also use their statements of values and codes of conduct as vehicles for attracting the right stakeholders to them.

Directors should, therefore, ensure that their corporation's strategy contains a statement of the values which they consider to be important for the harmonious and ethical running of their operations.

15. Does the strategy contain S.M.A.R.T. objectives that are well formulated and well stated?

Organizations use **objectives** to translate, measure and judge their progress in achieving *the goals embedded in their mission, vision and values*. These objectives may be of a qualitative or quantitative nature.

Quantitative objectives typically deal with expected "deliverables" that can be counted, such as financial results or other 'outcome activities' such as market share or stock price. **Qualitative objectives**, on the other hand, deal with stakeholders' opinions and feelings. However, these must also be expressed numerically (such as a customer satisfaction score). As a general rule, objectives should be established for each goal *contained within the organization's mission, vision and values*.

For example, one of the goals contained in a corporation's mission was to "provide the highest quality and service experience that consistently exceeds customer expectations." The organization decided to measure its progress towards achieving that goal through various surveys of its customers with the objective of scoring a 4.5 (or higher) out of 5 on customer satisfaction ratings.

To be effective, though, an organization's objectives must be both well formulated and well stated. These are known as S-M-A-R-T objectives:

✓ Specific (there is no ambiguity as to what the organization is trying to accomplish)
✓ Measurable (it is possible to determine whether the objectives have been achieved or not)
✓ Acceptable (the measures selected for tracking progress against the mission, vision and values are perceived as fair and appropriate)
✓ Realistic (they reflect reality and are motivational—i.e., capable of spurring commitment from employees and others), and
✓ Timely (as the great economist, Lord Keynes, once said: "In the long run, we are all dead!")

Regarding this last point, detailed organizational objectives are best stated for a time period of one to three years. They should also be revised at the end of each year as new information becomes available.

Also, determining whether an objective is realistic or not involves considerable judgment and skill. A key concern, therefore, is whether the people who will be responsible for achieving the specific targets contained in the objectives perceive those targets to be appropriate and motivational. To do this, directors first need to understand the basis upon which the objectives were established (e.g., customer/employee surveys, comparative competitive positioning, benchmarking studies, etc.) They must also determine whether the objectives **balance** the conditions in the external environment (especially the performance of competitors) with the organization's internal capabilities (for a further discussion of this, see question 16).

Organizational surveys asking how well high-level objectives are *known*, *understood*, and *accepted* by employees at each level are also useful to directors in determining the reasonableness of the objectives. After all, when people feel connected to their organization's strategic objectives, they typically work more diligently towards achieving those objectives and are more committed to the organization. This is called "employee engagement."

Finally, directors should assure themselves that the corporation's objectives are effectively aligned throughout the organization—especially to the front line. To be sure, with multiple S.M.A.R.T. objectives to be achieved, this can be a time consuming and daunting exercise the first time it is attempted. Accordingly, it may be best to phase in the alignment of objectives over time.

If you have boarded the wrong train, it is of no use running along the corridor in the opposite direction.

—Anon.

16. Are the "business arenas" specified in the coporation's strategy the right ones?

Corporations should strive to focus their resources **only** on those business arenas (i.e. products, services, customers, markets) where:

✓ favourable external market conditions exist for the corporation to achieve its stated mission, vision and values (this is called an 'opportunity') *and*
✓ the corporation has the internal resources—either on hand or quickly available—to pursue and capture the opportunity.

If either or both of these conditions do not exist, the corporation faces the difficult challenge of determining *if and how* the situation might be turned around and made more favourable or whether to seek greener pastures! Alternatively, it may even have to acknowledge the brutal reality that the organization is no longer sustainable and should be wound up.

This is the *essential discipline* that boards need to apply when assessing their corporation's strategy.

Making "business arena" selections is generally regarded as one of the most demanding—and important—processes in formulating or evaluating an organization's strategy. It involves the most amount of information gathering and typically represents the bulk of where strategic planning efforts should be placed.

Asking the following questions *for each business arena* will help directors assess their external market potential and internal capabilities:

✓ What is the nature and extent of demand for the products and/or services offered?

✓ What is the potential for profit?

✓ To what extent, and in what way, are customer needs currently being met by existing competitors?

✓ To what extent are the corporation's products and/or services significantly differentiated from—and offer a clear distinction over—those of existing competitors?

✓ Does the corporation have the resources, skills and capabilities required to meet the potential demand that has been identified in its business arena selections?

✓ If it lacks a distinctive advantage or any specific resources, skills and capabilities, is the corporation able to acquire the advantage/resources it needs, either on its own or in collaboration or partnership with others?

✓ What are the major assumptions underlying the choice of each major business arena selection?

✓ What is the relative importance of each business arena selection?

✓ What are the methods of entry to or exit from the major business arenas selected (i.e., merger, acquisition, divestment, closure, sale, etc.)?

✓ What alternative business 'postures' (i.e., grow/invest, hold, harvest, divest, no entry) were considered and rejected for each business arena (both existing and new)?

Strategy Execution Considerations

17. Have the proper organizational arrangements been selected, designed and aligned to reflect, reinforce and support the corporation's strategy?

Given sufficient time, information and human intelligence, *any* organization is capable of designing an outstanding strategy. The tough part occurs when it comes to executing it—i.e, *turning the strategy into a reality*. In fact, according to a study by *Fortune Magazine*, 90% of

companies fail to execute their strategies successfully. Boards, therefore, have the right and responsibility to be concerned about execution.

One of the major ways in which execution happens is through the corporation's operating plan. But, directors are generally discouraged from becoming involved in this area and for good reason (See the discussion related to Question 9).

The other major method by which corporations execute their strategies is by aligning their employees, structures and control systems to focus on, support and reinforce the organization's strategic goals and objectives. See Figure 2. This is called **strategic organizational alignment** and it entails four major considerations of concern to directors.

First, the mission, vision, values and objectives must be translated and expressed in terms that are meaningful and understood by ALL members of the organization. This is necessary if they are to put forward a united and concerted effort towards realizing the strategy. Often, this will require redefining or re-specifying employees' jobs in a way that *reflects the strategy's requirements*. The goal is to make sure the work of each employee addresses and contributes to the aims and aspirations contained in the strategy. These particular alignment activities should be conducted at least annually.

Second, individuals to be hired by the corporation should be recruited primarily on the basis of their ability to perform the critical tasks and priorities *specified in the strategy*. And when the strategy has changed, existing employees should be retrained or relocated to better align their skills and activities with it.

Third, information systems should be adjusted to regularly measure and report on the corporation's progress against all aspects of its strategy (especially the S.M.A.R.T. objectives) as well as the contributions individual members make towards its achievement. After all, timely, accurate and *"strategy focused" information* is necessary if the organization is to be able to assess the effectiveness of its operating plans and individuals' specific job behaviours—and then modify them, if necessary, to better achieve the strategy before it's too late.

Finally, the fourth element of organizational alignment demands that the corporation adjust its recognition systems so that employees are acknowledged and rewarded ONLY for the "right" efforts—i.e., *those that contribute to helping the organization realize its strategy*. Interestingly, recognizing people in this manner inspires and motivates them to put even greater efforts into making the strategy happen.

When key organizational structures and systems have been **aligned** with the strategy *and each other* as depicted in Figure 2, the probability of a corporation achieving its strategic goals and objectives will be greatly enhanced. Boards should confirmed that this has occured through a **Strategy-Execution Audit**™. (For an insightful and novel understanding of how organizations can easily create the kind of

The execution of the laws is more important than the making of them.

—**Thomas Jefferson, 3rd President of the United States**

organizational alignment needed for better success at implementing their missions, readers are encouraged to consider the #1 best selling book, *A Tale of Two Employees and the person who wanted to lead them*—also by the author. Readers will also find it useful visiting http://CorporateMissionsInc.com)

FIGURE 2

Achieving Excellence in Strategic Execution through High Organizational Alignment (2)

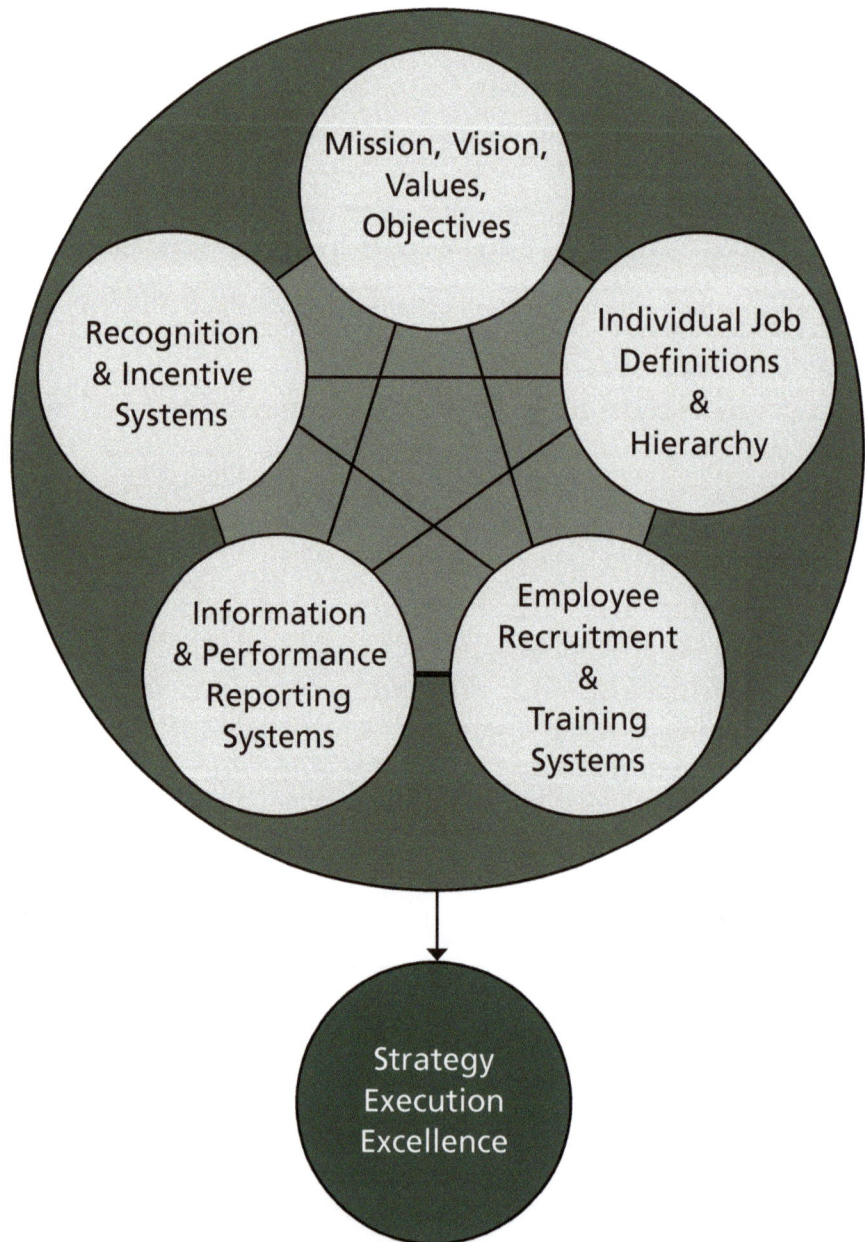

2. This is a unique framework developed by the author after years of research on how organizations turn their mission, vision, values and strategic objectives into reality. It is more formally referred to as 'the "Bart Star Strategy Execution Framework'. More information on how to execute a company's strategy can be found at: http://CorporateMissionsInc.com.

Assessing Strategic Risks

18. Have all the significant internal and external strategic risks facing the corporation been identified, quantified and addressed in the strategic plan?

With any strategy, some *uncertainty* always exists around its ultimate attainment.

And with uncertainty comes *risk*—i.e. possible events that, should they occur, would adversely affect the corporation and its ability to achieve its objectives. Some risks have a greater likelihood of occurring than others, but the presence of any of them can significantly alter the opportunities the organization is able to pursue, the weaknesses it is trying to overcome, the way certain organizational arrangements are made or the success the organization has in achieving objectives related to its mission, vision and values.

For this reason, company directors must be sure they understand all of the risks associated with a particular strategy, the *probability* or likelihood of these risks occurring and the *potential impact* each risk may have on the corporation. One way of doing this is by ensuring that the organization has in place an effective risk management system that identifies, measures and monitors known risks, estimates their impact, mitigates their occurrence or effect (e.g., through insurance, avoidance, codes of conduct or assigned risk managers), and identifies emerging dangers.

Another useful way for managing risks occurs as a result of the method by which directors are chosen to serve on the board. When correctly screened and selected, the individual and collective experiences and backgrounds of the directors provide a boardroom context in which they can properly understand, assess and help mitigate the risks facing their organizations.

Corporations, of course, face many different types of potential risk. However, the main risks of concern to boards parallel those which are *related to and drive its strategy*. These include risks that:

- ✓ stated objectives will not be realized
- ✓ opportunities perceived to exist with respect to realizing the mission, vision, values and objectives will not materialize (e.g. due to changes in customer demand or satisfaction levels, commodity prices, competitive intensity, regulations, government, environmental sensitivity, etc.)
- ✓ internal resources necessary to realize the strategy will either disappear or cannot reasonably be secured (e.g., the loss of key employees, a decline in organization morale, the inability to

The first step in the risk management process is to acknowledge the reality of risk. Denial is a common tactic that substitutes deliberate ignorance for thoughtful planning.

—Charles Tremper

innovate, a failure of marketing initiatives, the occurrence of fraud and asset theft, etc.)

✓ the compensation structure will increase the potential for unintended risk taking by management, and

✓ organizational arrangements chosen to implement the strategy do not function as intended.

Each of these risks should be spelled out and prioritized in the strategic plan. And, directors should approve only those strategies where the associated risks—and their impact—are considered to be tolerable *given the potential for success.*

Monitoring Progress

19. Are appropriate mechanisms in place to provide the board with timely feedback on the corporation's progress against its strategy, the underlying causes of any performance variance and any changes in the internal/ external environments or risk factors which would cause the board to consider altering the organization's strategy?

Once the corporation's strategy is approved and its supporting operational plan begins to be implemented, directors have a responsibility for monitoring the organization's *progress in achieving its strategic objectives.* Consequently, a review of the organization's progress against each of its strategic objectives—together with an update on any significant risks— should be undertaken regularly during meetings of the full board.

Another Word About 'Constructive Involvement' and Who Does What

According to the OECD:

"Corporate governance is the system by which business corporations are directed and controlled. The corporate governance structure specifies the distribution of rights and responsibilities among different participants in the corporation, such as, the Board, managers, shareholders, and other stakeholders, and spells out the rules and procedures for making decisions on corporate affairs." April 1999.

The board's responsibility to *actively participate* in developing and approving their organization's overall strategy, monitoring the

strategy's progress, and overseeing and guiding the organization are **quintessential activities of good governance**—whether for-profit or not-for-profit.

Many corporate boards have already made this transition. Others may only be beginning to take on these tasks and duties. As they do, it will create a shift both in their role and the manner in which they interact with management—especially the CEO.

As this document has described, senior executives have an important role to play in developing a corporation's strategy—but it is not an exclusive role. Good boards and their managements, therefore, must reach a common agreement on the responsibilities of each, since it is in no one's best interests if the relationship between the board and senior management becomes adversarial—especially when setting the organization's future direction.

Boards, therefore, should work diligently to create a positive relationship with management and, to assess this, need to ask:

20. Is our board constructively involved in the corporation's strategy?

A first step in building a relationship of constructive involvement with management is for the board to have an open and candid discussion with the CEO (and other members of senior management) about the governance responsibilities the board requires in terms of the organization's strategy. Ultimately, the board and management must come to an understanding and agreement as to:

- ✓ who does what, in terms of formulating, assessing and approving the corporation's strategy and strategic plan
- ✓ what areas constitute strategic—or board—decisions, and
- ✓ what areas represent operational/tactical—or management—decisions.

All of these responsibilities should be spelled out in a **Board Charter**.

Senior managers especially need to understand that the board's tasks with respect to strategy are not being taken because of a lack of confidence in the corporation's leadership. Rather, they are part of the **stewardship role** that all boards are being asked to perform to avoid the two major governance mistakes of the past: boards that either 'rubber stamped' major management decisions (especially the organization's strategy) or tried to "micro manage" the organization's operations.

Constructive involvement ultimately depends on the existence of a level of trust and mutual respect between the board and senior management. Corporate directors must feel comfortable in asking strategic questions. And senior management must feel that they can be forth-coming in their responses to those questions.

Consequently, corporate boards should conduct an **annual self-assessment** in the area of constructive involvement, possibly with a skilled facilitator, to help directors assess the degree of trust and respect that exists between them and management and to help sort out mutual responsibilities. Ideally, this should be part of a complete board governance assessment or review. And to the extent that problem areas are identified, the board could then consider what steps it next needs to take in order to correct the situation.

Strategic Plans and Planning

A **Strategic Plan** is a document that records decisions made by the corporation with respect to its future strategy, including the rationales, analysis and background information that support those decisions. Good strategic planning processes facilitate the creation of a superior strategy and ensure that the appropriate information is contained in the plan. Information typically included in a strategic plan includes:

Vision, Mission and Values

S.M.A.R.T. Objectives (related to the mission, vision and values)

Major Business Arenas (for achieving the mission, vision, values and objectives)

External Environmental Analysis to assess the potential for achieving the S.M.A.R.T. objectives in selected business arenas

- ✓ Political, economic, technological, environmental and social demographics analysis
- ✓ Market research (formal and/or informal) **related to** identifying and satisfying (current and unmet) stakeholder (i.e., investor, customer, and societal) needs
- ✓ Potential 'target market' demand/growth/profitability
- ✓ Number and type of competitors
- ✓ Relative positioning of competitors and their degree of product/ service differentiation
- ✓ Barriers to entry/exit
- ✓ 'Switching costs' related to customers and suppliers

"Unless a variety of opinions are laid before us, we have no opportunity of selection, but are bound of necessity to adopt the particular view which may have been brought forward"

—Herodotus, 5th century BC

- ✓ Nature and degree of customer and supplier dependencies
- ✓ Industry benchmarks and performance standards

Internal Resource Analysis to assess the corporation's ability to achieve its S.M.A.R.T. objectives in selected business arenas

- ✓ Strengths and weaknesses analysis **related to** achieving goals and objectives and increasing competitive advantage
- ✓ Analysis of capabilities for innovation
- ✓ Investor/analyst satisfaction survey results
- ✓ Customer satisfaction survey results
- ✓ Employee satisfaction survey results
- ✓ Gap analysis results relative to desired 'outcomes'
- ✓ Key success factors
- ✓ Plans for overcoming critical weaknesses or strengthening advantages

Methods of entry into (or exit from) major business arenas and domain selections

- ✓ Merger /acquisition
- ✓ Joint venture
- ✓ Strategic alliance
- ✓ Divestment/closure/sale

Risk Analysis

- ✓ Major risks (internal and external)
- ✓ Risk impact analysis e.g. sensitivity analysis
- ✓ Risk impact outcomes—including best and worst cases
- ✓ Risk management/abatement tactics

Assumptions

- ✓ Qualitative
- ✓ Quantitative

Major Strategic Alternatives

- ✓ A summary of major changes represented in the proposed/future strategy in relation to the strategy currently in use
- ✓ Descriptions of major strategic alternatives that were rejected and the rationale for their rejection

Rationales

- ✓ rationales for the proposed strategy—i.e., how the proposed/ future strategy will optimize the achievement of objectives in accordance with the mission, vision, and values.

Strategic Organizational Alignment/Strategy Implementation

- ✓ Organization chart
- ✓ Major changes in job definitions, information systems, and human resource practices in order to bring them into alignment with the strategy
- ✓ Succession plan for key management/board positions
- ✓ Potential areas of resistance to change—and methods for overcoming them
- ✓ Links between the strategic and operating plans

Financial and other measurements

- ✓ The projected financial impact of the proposed/future strategy for at least 3 years.
- ✓ Key performance indicators
- ✓ Milestones

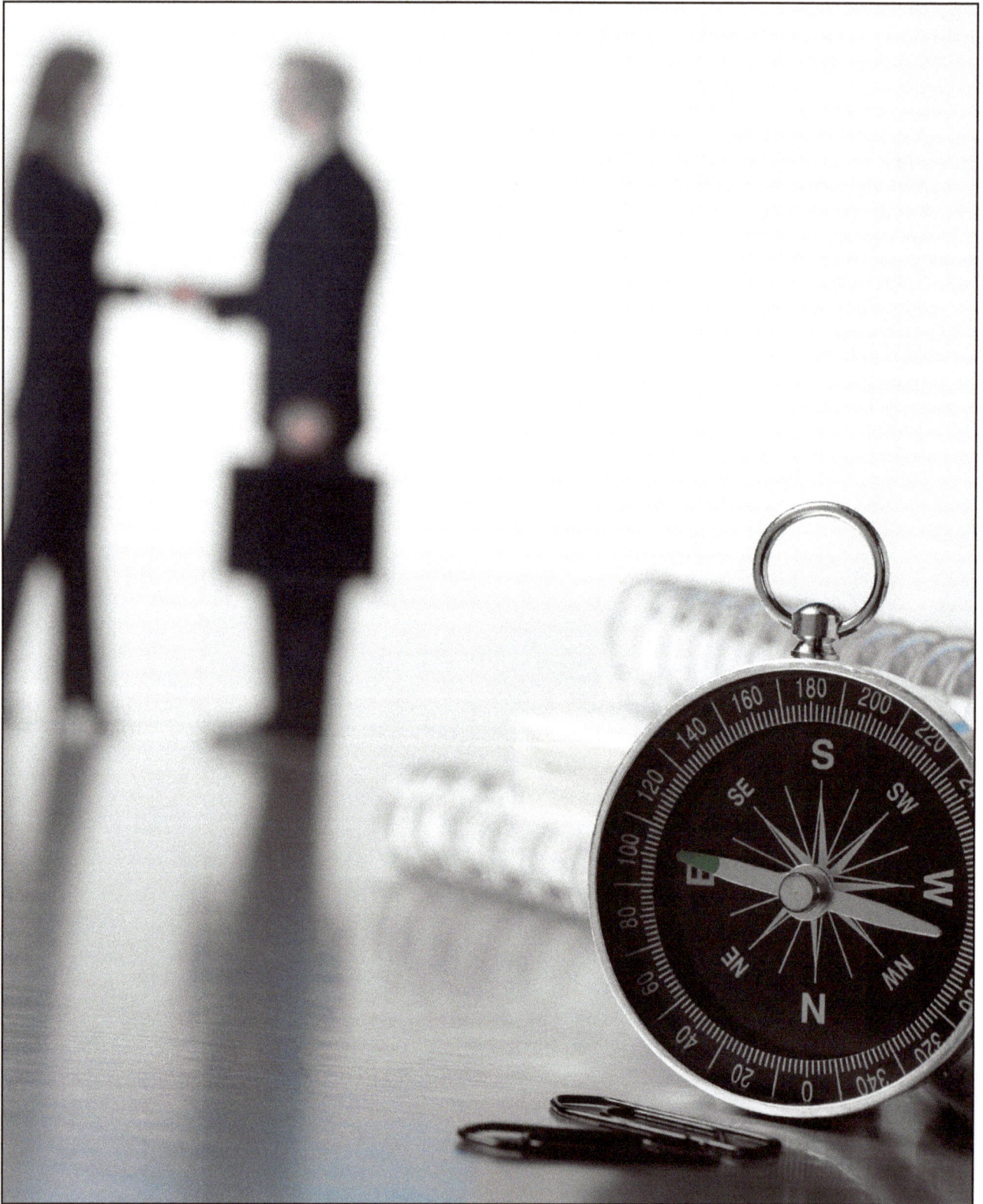

20 Essential Questions Workbook

On the following pages, you'll find the 20 questions with space for you to write your own response. Feel free to photocopy these pages so that you can update them from time to time.

1. How is strategy defined at this corporation?
2. What are we ultimately trying to accomplish (currently)—or where do we eventually want to get to? (The Vision Goal)
3. What is our current purpose—or, why do we exist? (The Mission Goals)
4. What are the current internal ethical and cultural ("how we do things around here") priorities that attract stakeholders to us? (The Values Goals)
5. What are the specific measures and targets that we currently use to judge our progress in achieving our vision, mission and values goals? (The Objectives)
6. What specific products and/or services have we currently chosen to focus on and, to which specific customers (or markets) have we chosen to offer them for the purposes of achieving our objectives? (The Business Arenas)
7. Is the definition and interpretation of the word "strategy", as described above in Questions 1 to 6, shared by all directors and management?
8. What are the major business strategies that make up the overall corporate strategy?
9. Do circumstances warrant the board's involvement in (i.e. reviewing, assessing and approving) the corporation's detailed operating plan?
10. Does this corporation have the right strategy and, if not, what should it be?
11. What process was used to formulate the strategy contained in the corporation's strategic plan and does the plan's document contain all of the proper information?
12. Does the strategy have the right vision?
13. Does the strategy have the right mission?
14. Does the strategy have a proper statement of values?
15. Does the strategy contain S.M.A.R.T. objectives that are well formulated and well stated?
16. Are the "business arenas" specified in the corporation's strategy the right ones?
17. Have the proper organizational arrangements been selected, designed and aligned to reflect, reinforce and support the corporation's strategy?
18. Have all the significant internal and external strategic risks facing the corporation been identified, quantified and addressed in the strategic plan?
19. Are appropriate mechanisms in place to provide the board with timely feedback on the corporation's progress against its strategy, the underlying causes of any performance variance and any changes in the internal/external environments or risk factors which would cause the board to consider altering the organization's strategy?
20. Is our board constructively involved in the corporation's strategy?

1. How is strategy defined at this corporation?

_____

_____

_____

_____

2. What are we ultimately trying to accomplish (currently)—or where do we eventually want to get to? (The Vision Goal)

_____

_____

_____

_____

3. What is our current purpose—or, why do we exist? (The Mission Goals)

_____

_____

_____

_____

4. What are the current internal ethical and cultural ("how we do things around here") priorities that attract stakeholders to us? (The Values Goals)

_____

_____

_____

5. What are the specific measures and targets that we use to judge our progress in achieving our vision, mission and values goals? (The Objectives)

_____

_____

_____

_____

6. What specific products and/or services have we currently chosen to focus on and, to which specific customers (or markets) have we chosen to offer them for the purposes of achieving our objectives? (The Business Arenas)

_____

_____

_____

_____

7. Is the definition and interpretation of the word "strategy", as described above in Questions 1 to 6, shared by all directors and management?

_____

_____

_____

_____

8. What are the major business strategies that make up the overall corporate strategy?

_____

_____

_____

_____

9. Do circumstances warrant the board's involvement in (i.e. reviewing, assessing and approving) the corporation's detailed operating plan?

_____

_____

_____

_____

10. Does this corporation have the right strategy and, if not, what should it be?

_____

_____

_____

_____

11. What process was used to formulate the strategy contained in the corporation's strategic plan and does the plan's document contain all of the proper information?

_____

_____

_____

_____

12. Does the strategy have the right vision?

_____

_____

_____

_____

13. Does the strategy have the right mission?

_____

_____

_____

_____

14. Does the strategy have a proper statement of values?

_____

_____

_____

_____

15. Does the strategy contain S.M.A.R.T. objectives that are well formulated and well stated?

_____

_____

_____

_____

_____

16. Are the "business arenas" specified in the corporation's strategy the right ones?

_____

_____

_____

_____

_____

17. Have the proper organizational arrangements been selected, designed and aligned to reflect, reinforce and support the corporation's strategy?

_____

_____

_____

_____

_____

18. Have all the significant internal and external strategic risks facing the corporation been identified, quantified and addressed in the strategic plan?

_____

_____

_____

_____

_____

19. Are appropriate mechanisms in place to provide the board with timely feedback on the corporation's progress against its strategy, the underlying causes of any performance variance and any changes in the internal/external environments or risk factors which would cause the board to consider altering the organization's strategy?

_____

_____

_____

_____

_____

20. Is our board constructively involved in the corporation's strategy?

_____

_____

_____

_____

47

About the Author

Dr. Chris Bart, FCA is the **world's leading authority** on organizational mission and vision statements. He is the **Founder**, **Principal and Lead Professor of The Directors College at McMaster University**, Canada's first university accredited corporate director certification program. Dr. Bart is also the author of the Canadian business #1 best seller, *A Tale of Two Employees and the Person Who Wanted to Lead Them* as well as the widely acclaimed publication *20 Essential Questions Directors of Not-for-profit Organizations Should Ask About Strategy*.

Through his pioneering research and teachings, Dr. Bart has become highly sought after by organizations seeking to develop vision and mission statements that get results. His practical approach for bringing mission statements to life has inspired business leaders and audiences around the world.

As a **Professor of Strategic Market Leadership (Strategy and Governance)** at McMaster University's DeGroote School of Business, Dr. Bart has published over 100 articles, cases and reviews. He currently serves as **Associate Editor** of the International Journal of Business Governance & Ethics. He is also an **innovator**. He helped establish the Management of Innovation and New Technology Research Centre (MINT~RC) at McMaster and was its first Director. Later, he devised and created the Innovation Management Network; a worldwide association of academics and practitioners who collaborate through the internet on matters of innovation and new technology.

Dr. Bart has been awarded the **Ontario Chamber of Commerce "Outstanding Business Achievement Award for Corporate Governance"**, the **Hamilton Chamber of Commerce "HR Hero Award"**, the **United Way "Chairman's Award"**, the **Human Resources Professionals Association "Summit Award for Corporate Governance & Strategic Leadership"**, **McMaster's "Innovation Award"** and the **Queen Elizabeth II Diamond Jubilee Medal**. For his research, he has received both the McMaster **Research Recognition Award** and its

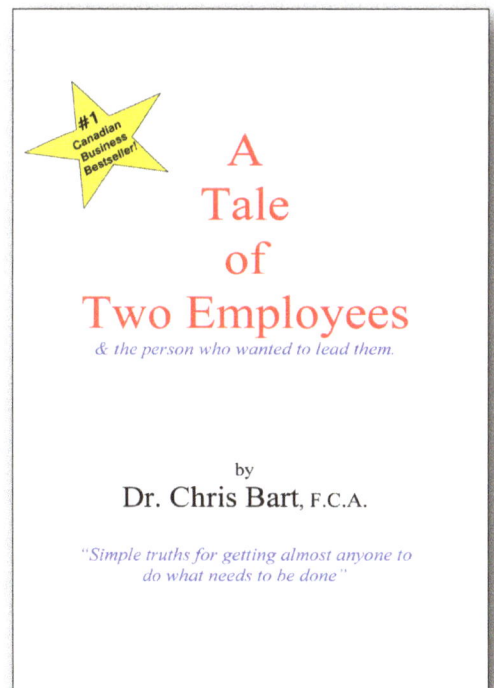

#1 Canadian Business Bestseller!

A
Tale
of
Two Employees
& the person who wanted to lead them.

by
Dr. Chris Bart, F.C.A.

"Simple truths for getting almost anyone to do what needs to be done"

Theory to Practice Award. A highly regarded lecturer, Dr. Bart has received both the "**Outstanding Undergraduate Business Professor**" and "**MBA Professor of the Year**" awards on multiple occasions. He has also won "**The President's Award for Teaching Excellence**", McMaster's highest teaching award—which made him the most decorated professor at the DeGroote School. In 2009, his CA designation was elevated to **FCA** (Fellow of the Institute of Chartered Accountants).

Over the years, Dr. Bart has been invited to lecture at numerous institutions throughout the world, including South Africa, Switzerland, the United Kingdom, Australia, the Czech Republic and China.

Dr. Bart is listed in **Canadian Who's Who** and has been a director on many Boards.

Dr. Chris Bart, FCA
Corporate Missions, Inc.
chrisbart@corporatemissionsinc.com
(905)-515-6399
www.corporatemissionsinc.com

www.ingramcontent.com/pod-product-compliance
Lightning Source LLC
Chambersburg PA
CBHW040146200326
41519CB00035B/7613